Obadiah Cyrus Auringer

Scythe and Sword

Poems

Obadiah Cyrus Auringer

Scythe and Sword
Poems

ISBN/EAN: 9783744705264

Printed in Europe, USA, Canada, Australia, Japan

Cover: Foto ©Thomas Meinert / pixelio.de

More available books at **www.hansebooks.com**

SCYTHE AND SWORD

POEMS

BY

O C AURINGER

BOSTON

D LOTHROP COMPANY

FRANKLIN AND HAWLEY STREETS

1887

TO

EDWARD EGGLESTON, D.D.,

WARM FRIEND

AND WISE COUNSELLOR,

THESE POEMS ARE AFFECTIONATELY DEDICATED

BY

THE AUTHOR.

.

CONTENTS.

SCYTHE AND SWORD.

THE ORCHARD.

I.

THE orchard stretches from the door,
 To right and left and far along,
To where the gray fence winds before
 The slope where meadow grasses throng.

The trunks, like graven columns old,
 Rise from the tight turf all arow,
And breaking into arms uphold
 A roof of emerald and snow.

Its breezy floor with gold is strown,
 As thick as stars on cloudless night,
Where flower-enamored Spring has sown
 Her dandelions for delight.

Adown the long aisles careless pass
  The wavering butterflies of May,
And on the spreading mat of grass
  In troops the fitful shadows play.

II.

Midway along the deep arcade
  The monarch of the orchard stands,
For fifty years through light and shade
  The glory of the homestead lands.

His massive trunk is straight and free,
  His great arms of heroic brawn
Are spread abroad in majesty
  O'er many a rood of level lawn.

His leaf is greenest emerald,
  His bloom is mottled blood and snow,
His fruit is mellow globes of gold,
  With summer's choicest wines aglow.

The tufted sod about his feet
  At morn is longest wet with dew,

So close the leafy branches meet,
  So rare the rifts the sun shines through.

Above his old root swells a mound,
  A royal pillow for the head
Of one who on the fragrant ground
  Would lie and dream as on a bed.

'T is here at noon's celestial hour,
  When not with spirit weighed and worn,
But fresh and open as a flower,
  Through which all wandering airs are borne,

I come.   Beneath the rustling tide
  Of leaves I lie upon the grass,
While winds of heaven from far and wide
  Blow me a greeting as they pass.

The farmer sun, whose harvest face
  The cloud of foliage shuts from view,
Finds here and there unguarded space
  To shoot a shining message through.

I feel the swift pulse of delight
  That thrills the wild bird on the wing;

My spirit, in the joys of flight,
   Joins his exultant caroling.

That wandering flower of groves and fields,
   The butterfly, luxurious guest,
To me his dainty secret yields;
   I join him in his foolish quest.

The pleasure-hunting bumblebee,
   Sipping from clover-cups his wine,
I apprehend, — I am as he,
   And all his honeyed thoughts are mine.

Ah! sweet wild friends of summer-time,
   By kindly love familiar made,
That in the day's delicious prime
   Throng round me, and are not afraid!

III.

Then hovering round me, lo! I hear
   Seraphic voices, tongue on tongue,
In airy syllables as clear
   As e'er through brain of poet rung.

Swift fade the fields, the birds grow mute,
   The winds fall faint and die away,
Soft sounds, as of a lyre or lute,
   With voices, o'er my spirit stray.

They speak to me sublimer things
   Than seer or master ever taught,
Or mind has gleaned in wanderings
   Through all the universe of thought.

The treasures of the secret place
   The passive soul may freely share,
While he that runs with ardent pace
   Comes baffled back, and in despair.

So in a trance I lie and hear
   That hidden stream in music flow,
Whose happy current, still and clear,
   Sweeps brightly round our walls of woe.

I rise as one by magic birth
   'Mong new-created things set free,
To look upon a wondrous earth
   'Neath skies of stainless purity.

It lies in floods of heaven immersed :
Gone is the curse, the sin, the stain ;
And glorious, as at the first,
Man walks in joy with God again.

A WIND SONG.

Blow, freely blow,
　　Over the snow, O wind!
As merrily blow o'er the hills of snow
　　As if never a man had sinned,
As if never a woman had wept,
　　Or a delicate child grown pale,
Or a maiden's warm tears crept
　　To hallow a faithless tale!

Blow, stoutly blow,
　　Strong in thy heathen joy!
Sorrow thou surely canst not know,
　　For thine is the heart of a boy!
For thine is the freedom and strength
　　Of a rover careless and gay,
Over the fair land's length
　　Joyfully wandering away!

Blow, bravely blow,
　　Out of the fields of air!
Till we see thy garments' airy flow,
　　And the gleam of thy flying hair;

Till the light of thy broad bright wing
And thy glad eyes set us free,
And we feel in our hearts the spring
Of a joy that was wont to be!

THE VALE OF SPIRITS.

In deep green woods there lies a fairy glade
  Shut in by tawny hemlocks wild and tall;
  Its floor is laid with richest moss, and all
Its round is steeped in most delicious shade.
It is a spot for listening silence made;
  Few sounds awake it, save the wild-bird's call,
  And winds that murmur round its forest wall,
Like instruments at airy distance played.

'Tis there a still and stolen guest I lie,
  And listen to the weird wood-spirits singing;
I hear their bell-like voices floating nigh,
  From arches green and dewy dingles springing;
They pass in elfin song and laughter by,
  I hear their clear ha! ha! in deep dells ringing.

THE OLD BALSAM.

YEAR in, year out, unchanged thou standest there,
    And broodest in a visionary wise;
Inscrutably the same in seasons rare
    As 'midst the winter's straits and stormy cries.

Solemn and vast, and hard in reticence,
    That speaks not save in unremembered tongue,
Thou standest an enigma and offence,
    Steadfast and old 'midst all that's frail and
    young.

Looking on noble mountains from thy place,
    And on still waters stayed in linkéd hills, —
A landscape with a chance capricious face,
    Now charmed with smiles, now vexed with winter
    ills.

Alternate barrenness, bloom, snow, and flowers,
    Web sunbeam and frost crystal, now and then;
All things in turn, and flowing like the hours,
    And neighbored by the near abodes of men.

'Midst these, and under skies as fair as joy,
  Or hard as hate, and drawn in fierce distress,
Thou keep'st the calm that nothing can annoy,
  The mark — the state no chance can dispossess.

For why? what art thou, and from whence, that so
  Thou lettest pass the ineffectual world,
Scornful of its vext strivings to and fro, —
  Sea without port, whose sails are nowhere furled?

What art thou, with such matchless hardihood,
  That keep'st thy spirit while the fiery sway
Of change unsettles e'en the brave and good,
  And leaves not one, but whirls them all away?

Art thou a prophet, like of old, with feet
  Set steadfast on the ancient base of things,
With mighty heart of uncorrupted heat,
  Whose thoughts are strong, fierce angels clad with
    wings?

A living sign whereon the world shall gaze,
  And be reproved for its inconstancy,
Confronting all its feeble pride of days
  With the calm purpose of eternity?

I think thou art a prophet; yet thou hast
    At sudden times a glow of milder grace,
That mellows o'er that mood, — that iron cast
    Of thought, which marks thee of prophetic race,

Like moonlight over armor; and at night,
    Oft when sleep drugs the vulgar sense with
        dreams,
Thou wear'st a look of rapture, and a light
    Of elfish wildness round thy figure gleams.

Sad, yet withal not lonely, but as one,
    For his high heart exalted like a star,
Cut off from kin, and understood by none,
    Thou hast thy precious visits from afar.

Ere fields revive their green at Spring's behest,
    Robin, the orator from out the south,
From the precarious vantage of thy crest
    Pleads loud his cause with eloquence of mouth.

The meteor oriole, of golden fame,
    After all woods and orchards overflown,
Cools in thy ample cloud his heart of flame,
    And plies the art so wondrously his own.

The lady bluebird, quaint and delicate,
    And yellowbird the fairy, still and small,
Have known thee long for some congenial trait, —
    Some grace, some charm familiar over all.

In the black midnight, hark! a cry, a shout,
    As of a night sea roaring unto sea!
The lightning and the storm have found thee out,
    Thy giant kindred hold converse with thee!

For these thou hast a voice of speech, a tongue
    Confessed, or couched in mystic silences,
That ancient speech unchanged since time was
        young —
    Ah, how forgot of all save such as these!

Nay, not of all; — some few large hearts remain,
    Which heed the noble music nature makes,
Which rest and listen, rise and toil again,
    Strong in the joy its melody awakes.

Some sage, some prophet, surely thou must be,
    Since these esteem thee something more than
        friend;

Yea, mine own heart hath apprehended thee,
   Henceforth thou art my brother to the end!

A soul serene, that hath its dreams apart;
   A mind unmoved by blind Ambition's call;
A noble, calm capacity of heart;
   A faithful vision glorifying all.

Of strengths like these the present world hath need,
   If I, who question thee, have learned aright, —
To give to time men of heroic breed,
   And bring the old sublimities to light.

Ah, well, good night, brave friend; kind darkness
     keep
   This image of thee warm, which now I hold;
I go awhile to walk the paths of sleep,
   'Midst frailer forms and visions manifold.

ONE OF NATURE'S SURPRISES.

FIRST NOVEMBER.

How full of rare surprises nature is!
Not often — with the sun so far withdrawn
To southward at the waning of the year,
Leaving the earth, deserted of the glow
And fire and passion of his summer love,
To bide old Winter's cold, ungenial clasp —
Is felt so sweet and pleasant a surprise
As met me on a country road to-day.
Slowly I drove along, with eye alert,
And heart intent to catch the faintest gleam
Of glory fading from the autumn hills, —
To catch the last pathetic look of earth,
So full of sad regret for glories flown,
And vanished with the joys of summer-time, —
Sweet songs, rich feasts, and airs of paradise
Upon the desolation of her house ; —
To meet her farewell look, and hear the sigh,
Inaudible to all but charméd ears,
That at this sad and desolate time of year
Arises from her great forsaken heart,

Doomed, as she knows, soon to be pierced with
    frosts,
And frozen into stone a hundred days.
I rode along, when, lo! beside the way,
Beside a ruined fence patched green with moss,
And sunken down in dampness and decay;
'Midst tangled briars long blown bare of leaves,
And dried and withered by the autumn winds;
On frail, precarious stems, shrunk thin as thread—
Rare raspberries! as large and red and round
And full of rich suggestiveness as e'er
The roguish-hearted Summer scattered free
O'er plots unused, and nooks beside the way,
To catch the hearts of merry schoolward elves,
And cheat them to an hour's romp and glee.
Ripe raspberries! rare gift, this time of year,
From even Earth, great mother rich in gifts!
With heart amid regret surprised by hope,
I stopped, and picked, and ate,—ate joy and faith:
Joy at such miracle by nature wrought,
Faith in the unfailing richness of her store.

RAIN SONG FOR OCTOBER.

BEAT, rain,
Against the pane, —
O beat with a welcome, soothing sound;
Cool and sweet,
After the heat,
Welcome, O rain, to the dry and thirsty ground!

Sing, rain,
Amidst the grain, —
O sing to the grass and the parching sod!
Softly sing,
" Rejoice! I bring
Refreshing gifts for each little herb of God!"

Go, drouth,
Into the south, —
O fly to the desert, where no man is!
Go and stay
Under the ray
Of the red fierce sun in the lifeless wastes of his!

Praise, rain,
Our God again,
O praise him who gave thee a voice to praise!
And praise him we
For sending thee
To give us hope of the coming fruitful days!

AFTER THE HARVEST.

THE scythe is rusting in the tree,
  The rake lies broken on the glade,
The mower in a revery
  Is stretched at ease within the shade.

A goodly man the mower is,
  With sinews tough as twisted rods,
A form of manly grace is his,
  A head as trenchant as a god's.

A man of thought; the harvest o'er,
  Its heats and triumphs left behind,
He rests, and gives himself once more
  To pleasures of the heart and mind.

Such pleasures! All the glorious skies,
  Their happy deeps, their hues, their forms
That float, are wonders to his eyes;
  He glories in their fires and storms.

The sweet green earth he deems most fair;
 He knows her moods of ease and toil;
He walks abroad, and everywhere
 Sees blessings springing from the soil.

The woods and pastures, near and far,
 To him their secrets yield; he knows
The shy spot where the berries are,
 The corner where the sweet mint grows.

His friendships lie on every hand,
 In man and cattle, bird and bee;
And he is wise to understand
 The language of the flower and tree.

The free air and the light he quaffs
 Are turned to sunshine in his veins;
His speech is cheer, and when he laughs
 Great nature's joy is in the strains.

For him the cloud shall break and pass,
 And show behind its shattered bars
The splendor of the fields and grass,
 The glory of the sky and stars.

THE FIRST PHEBE.

SWEET latest herald of the spring,
  Fresh from thy rest at nature's heart,
Where thou dost linger listening
  Till all her warm, strong pulses start.

Last eve I heard thy fairy note
  Along the orchard arches blown;
Faint, — faint it seemed, and far remote,
  And yet I knew it for thine own.

Though wild the robin sang above,
  And bluebird carolled blithe and clear,
Thy low voice, like the word of love,
  Found instant pathway to mine ear.

And in my breast the pulse of spring
  Beat out an answering throb; I knew
'Midst rivals' noisier carolling,
  The one fine voice of prophet true.

And thine, alas! a prophet's fate;
　All night the rains have fallen on thee;
All night no comfort, — no, but hate,
　Darkness and doubt and misery.

Thou comest not to me this morn
　With secrets of thy earth and air,
But with thy poor drowned wings forlorn,
　Thrice weary with thy heart's despair!

Where didst thou pass thy soul's unrest
　Through all those bitter hours and wild?
Behold thy soft sky-woven vest
　With darkest stains of earth defiled!

O welcome to my porch and vine,
　Thy singing-bower in other days!
Make it thy house wherein to pine,
　Which once thou mad'st thy house of praise!

Ay, welcome to my heart, dear bird!
　Come in, come in, and lodge with me:
This breast with greater griefs is stirred
　Than any fate can bring to thee.

I 'll tell thee of the wearing pain
　No human heart may share or know, —
The slow worm that amidst the grain
　Robs harvest of its overflow.

And thus with kindly sympathy
　We 'll sun these lives with sorrows sown,
Lest some approaching season see
　Their fields with bitter weeds o'ergrown.

See now the clouds flow back! the sun
　Comes through the orchard's eastern gate;
Adown the air fleet murmurs run,
　That break in song and soar elate.

The scenes that coldly viewed thy plight
　With golden lights are hallowed now;
The drops that beat on thee all night
　Are chains of diamonds on the bough.

CRICKET SONG.

SING to me, sing to me, sad and low,
  Cricket under the rafter;
Trill to me tenderly, mournfully; — O!
  More sweet than the lark's loud laughter
Is thy plaintive voice in the evening's glow,
  That follows the fierce hours after!

Sing to me, trill to me; — ah, my heart
  Lonely lies and forsaken,
Drooping in sorrowful silence apart,
  By tremulous grief o'ertaken,
And the voice is thine that can soothe its smart,
  Its tenderest hopes awaken.

Sing to me! — ah, for a heart like thine,
  Cricket under the rafter!
Then could I make all my sorrows divine
  That follow the fierce joys after!
I could sing, — I could sing, — and a song were
    mine
  More sweet than the wild lark's laughter!

TO A SUMMER EVENING WIND.

Soft wind of summer's eve,
  Fresh from blue fields and paradisial air,
Methinks in happy vision I perceive
  Thee winged with floating hair,

A spirit quaintly dight
  In robe of airiest gossamer outspread,
Roaming the earth in innocent delight,
  By wayward fancy led;

In sweet unconsciousness,
  Wafting thy cool delights through breathless
      ways,
That speak again in music, and confess
  Thy joys with grateful praise;

Waking with magic wings
  Life and fresh grace in tree and vine and flower,
Till all alive, with airy whisperings
  They fill the twilight hour.

Out of the deep land's breast
   A murmur comes, of many glad sounds made,
Gathered from lake and plain and mountain crest,
   And meadows bathed in shade;

A universal sigh
   Of calm content and gratitude to thee,
Who feignest not to listen, being shy,
   As such rare spirits be.

Through all the arid day
   Hast thou been sleeping sweetly in the hill,
Unseen by woodland fairies in their play,
   While all around was still;

Save when some hidden bird,
   Full of sly wildwood mischief, suddenly
Broke on thy dream 'mid foliage unstirred,
   In mocking melody,

Waking at quiet eve
   In most divine refreshment and delight
To bathe in air and over earth to weave
   Thy far erratic flight.

Thy light approach unreels
  A band of dancing dimples o'er the lake,
Such as on charméd nights the skimming keels
  Of fairies' shallops make.

Thy breath is in the vine,
  That half my window's prospect serves to screen ;
Ah ! are not those thy lovely eyes that shine
  The woven leaves between ?

Welcome, celestial guest !
  With what fond message comest thou to me, —
What secret gift of hope or rapture blest,
  Of all thy fair eyes see ?

Thou art so shy a sprite ! —
  Here ! breathe it through the vine into my ear !
From out the bosom of the deepening night
  Thy arch laugh answers clear.

Thou art not here nor there,
  Thou comest not at this or that one's call,
I know thee now, that thou art everywhere,
  Thy blessings free to all !

Ah! what a bliss to feel
  Thy cool breath o'er hot cheek and forehead play,
Delicious to the sense as airs that steal
  From flowery woods of May.

How pleasant to the ear
  Thy songs are, that their ceaseless music keep,
Soft — soft, like voices sleepy children hear
  Call from the shores of sleep.

FADING DAYS.

FILLED with a quiet sadness nigh to tears,
When tears come fresh from no ungentle spring,
Beside this stream, whose tongue runs faltering,
I watch this graceful fading of the year's.
A breeze shakes all the host of grassy spears,
Rustling their faded pennants where they cling,
A brown rust widens round the fairies' ring,
Pale on each bough a dying grace appears.
The air is tremulous with hovering fears,
Each moment some loved charm is taking wing;
For every pearl that falls from summer's string
Dies in my breast some song her love endears.
O autumn, haste! blow fresh through heart and brain
The riper notes of thy reviving strain!

GLEN LAKE AT TWILIGHT.

How still she lies !
A bride in all her wedding splendor dressed,
   After the day's sweet tumult and surprise
     Laid in soft rest.

  Ere yet the hour
Has come that brings the bridegroom to her arms,
   In that mysterious pause 'twixt bud and flower
     Of royal charms.

With dearest eyes
Closed over dreams of glorious substance wrought,
   Placid as peace, in all content she lies,
     And still as thought.

The tender flush
Of twilight lingering warm on brow and cheek,
   Upturned in perfect slumber 'mid the hush,
     Serene and meek.

Scarcely a gem
Is shaken 'midst the clusters on her breast,
 Nor trembles there the red rose on its stem,
  So deep her rest.

No faintest stir
Of zephyrs playing unseen round her bed,
 Disturbs the folds of the bright robe round her
  In wealth outspread.

'Twixt low hills peaked
Hangs the bepainted couch on which she lies,
 Pillowed with mist and curtained by the streaked,
  Delightful skies.

All life around
Gives worship in a silence delicate,
 Soothed by the vision and the charm profound
  Of peace so great.

 In white undress,
The moon, with two shy children at her side,
 Looks down on her in matron tenderness,
  Regret, and pride.

Tranquil and fair,
Untroubled by a thought of all the earth
She sleeps, secure in kindly nature's care
As at her birth.

From thee, still lake,
Passes the shadow of a peace unguessed
By all the dreamless world, substance to take
In this sure breast.

THE ROBE-WEAVERS.

UPON the hills they set their loom,
  They wove in silence in the night;
When morning smiled through mist and gloom
  Earth wore a robe of shining white.

It lay upon her rich and chaste,
  With starry jewels sprinkled o'er,
Above the one by floods defaced
  That yesterday she sadly wore.

Of stainless snow they wove it fair,
  And wrapped her in it close and deep;
They sowed it with frost-crystals rare,
  And left her lovely in her sleep.

And many and many a peerless dress
  They 've wrought in loving sympathy,
To keep her winter barrenness
  Clothed with perpetual purity.

    ' For on the hills, by night or day,
       By spirit hands her garments grow,
    Fast as the old ones wear away,
       Because the spirits love her so.

WINTER.

O WINTER! thou art not that haggard Lear,
With stormy beard and countenance of woe,
Raving amain, or dumbly crouching low,
In hoary desolation mocked with fear!
To me thou art the white queen of the year,
A stately virgin in her robes of snow,
With royal lilies crowned, and all aglow
With holy charms, and gems celestial clear.
Nor dost thou come in barren majesty, —
Thou hast thy dower of sunbeams, thrice refined, —
Nor songless, but with cheerful minstrelsy,
Rung from the singing harpstrings of the wind;
And, ah! with such sweet dreams, such visions
        bright,
Of flowers, and birds, and love's divine delight!

THE VOICE OF WATERS.

SINGER! by the lonely main,
Sitting on the sea-rocks hoary,
Listen to his ancient story,
Sung in deep-resounding strain.
From amid the endless flow
Of the tides that come and go;
Through the passion and the strife,
Stern and grand and sad as life, —
Sounds of anguish and of crying,
Sin's remorse and sorrow's sighing;
'Mid the noise and stormy strain
Of his sea-wrath launched amain,
Down the sun's red track that bridges
Long uprolling ocean ridges,
When his passion sinks subdued
Into golden quietude;
O'er the slumber great as peace,
Where his spirit finds release, —
In and through and over all
Hear the weird sea-voices call.
Listen while their strains come singing

Round thee, thought with music bringing,
Till the soul is born once more
Which the poets knew of yore,
'Midst the glorious pangs that earth
Feels at a diviner birth, —
Child whose restless cries shall be
Harpings of sublimity;
Whose imperial heart, imbrued
In the fires of solitude,
Wraps the scornful core intense
Of a fierce magnificence,
Worrying the parent breast
With his tumults of unrest.
He shall feed thy searching soul
With the long-delaying fire,
He shall wing thee for the goal
Of thy uttermost desire:
'T is the spirit of the sea
Gives the wings to Poesy.

THE UNTIMELY SINGER.

A BIRD with azure breast and beak of gold,
A joyous stranger, beautiful and shy,
Flown from far groves beneath a summer sky,
At morn amid our March woods bare and cold
Sang like a spirit. Raptures such as hold
The arches charmed, and hush the zephyr's sigh,
From his enamored throat flowed carelessly
In musical low warblings manifold.
At length he ceased, with arch head bent aside,
And listened long! but from the woodlands bare
No cheering voice of melody replied, —
Only a faint call from the fields of air;
Swiftly he rose, and as the echo died
Fled to the open heavens, and warbled there.

SONG'S DIVINITY.

ALL my singing seems divine
When the spirit, like a feather,
Floats 'mid sunny summer weather,
Buoyantly through shade and shine;
When my treasure-house of trees
Murmurs with the bartering bees;
And from meadows purpled over
With the royal flush of clover
Waves of sumptuous perfume rise,
Rolled in warmth of paradise,
Where the lark rides blithe and strong
Bubbling o'er with liquid song.
When in mossy spaces cool
Ripples quicken on the pool,
And the streams race in the sun,
Tossing diamonds as they run.
If with these and skies serene
Glimpsed through woven boughs of green,
On whose walls in azure laid
Airy figures form and fade;
And the wind in playful sallies

Whispering through the curtained alleys,
Wafting down the shaded walk
Voice of friends in pleasant talk, —
Then are all things sweet and fair,
Then the world is ruled aright,
And with heaven everywhere
Song is motion, air, and light,
Melody is poured like wine,
And my songs are all divine.

THE VOYAGERS.

'T is moonlight on the sea,
  Calmly the tides are sleeping;
In heaven far and free
  The stars their watch are keeping.

Softly our fairy boat
  Moves on with restful motion,
Like a snowy swan afloat,
  O'er the breast of the musing ocean.

Airs from a far-off sphere
  In the sky's wide quiet lying,
Waft us a chant of fear,
  In ethereal whispers dying.

The starry wrecks that float
  Down heaven's wild tide of glory,
O'er which ill angels gloat,
  Are the theme of their sad sea story.

The tender tones and sad
  Of the spirit winds remind us
Of the hours so calmly glad
  With the hearts we leave behind us.

Hint they in sighing song
  Of the dangers that enfold us,
And the weary days and long
  Ere the hills again behold us.

In vain the stars and wind
  With their voices that implore us;
The hills lie dim behind,
  And the ocean is before us.

The passionate dark isles
  Wooed us with promise golden,
But well we knew their wiles
  From tale and poem olden.

The glimmering sails went past,
  And the sailors sang us warning, —
"O whither away so fast!
  Come home to the port of morning!"

Fleet sails that homeward fly
  Storm-winds and waves shall sever;
The isles shall sink and die,
  But the sea rolls on forever!

Past are the storms that plague,
  And rocks that threat us grimly;
No more the wan fogs vague
  Oppress our vision dimly.

No more the siren's breath
  Shames the pure silence holy,
Fades her rank bower of death
  On wide horizon lowly.

The fleeting sails are flown,
  Like ocean shadows shifting,
And beneath the moon, alone,
  Our fairy boat is drifting.

Over the mute sea's wave,
  Over the sleeping billow,
No dreamy couch we crave,
  Long for no downy pillow.

SCYTHE AND SWORD.

Our hearts are on the deep,
  Our thoughts are with the ocean,
Our souls the wonder keep
  Of his silent, great emotion.

Softly the dying breeze
  Sinks on faint pinion failing;
Far o'er receding seas
  The reef's red flame is paling.

Faint, — faint the hills appear,
  That again shall know us never, —
A long fond look, a tear,
  And they are gone forever.

O rest! our voyage is o'er
  In the seas of danger haunted,
And we 'll sail forevermore
  The sea of the enchanted.

PRESAGE.

LIGHTLY, lightly glides our bark
  Over the moonlit sea!
Brightly, brightly burns the spark
  Of the lighthouse on our lee;
But away on the dim horizon's rim
  . Faint lights flash fitfully.

Brightly, brightly out of the blue
  The eloquent planets shine;
Lightly, lightly as ever it flew,
  The wind's wing fans the brine;
But low in the south, at the harbor's mouth,
  The kennelled storm-dogs whine.

Slowly, slowly fades the shore,
  Pale in the moonlight sleeping,
Lowly, lowly out before
  The jewelled sea is sweeping;
But far away in the outer bay
  The white foam-steeds are leaping.

Gently, gently rocks our boat
  Under the broad sails flowing,
Softly, softly round us float
  Voices of the night-wind blowing;
While the waves laugh low as they touch us and go,
  "Good night!" on their journey going.

Sweetly, sweetly floats a song
  Into the blue above;
Sweetly, sweetly, low and long,
  Singeth my lute-voiced love, —
My lily girl with her flesh of pearl,
  And her eyes like a brooding dove.

Sitting, sitting softly there
  Wrapped in her purity,
Sitting, sitting divinely fair
  In the trance of melody,
With the eager grace on her upturned face
  Of enchanted minstrelsy.

Fairer, fairer than the light
  Blossoms my lily pale;
Rarer, rarer than the night,

With its fainting visions frail;
But a spirit sits where the shadow flits
    In the corner of the sail.

Hiding, hiding closely here
    Out of the moon's broad eye;
Biding, biding close to my ear
    With a cunning art and sly,
Like a friend of ill my heart to chill
    With his truth that is a lie.

" Lovely, lovely in thy sight,
    Is the lily of thy desire;
Lovely, lovely as the night,
    But the night has a soul of fire;
And the lily may fold in her petals cold
    The flame of a passionate ire."

            .   .   .   .   .

Swiftly, swiftly flies our sail
·   Over the seething sea;
Wildly, wildly screams the gale,
    And the clouds flame wrathfully;
But high through the dark burns the steady spark
    Of the lighthouse on our lee.

INLAND.

On the bare cliffs in lonely revery
   I wait, and hear far off the smothered shocks
   Of billows plunging on the stubborn rocks
That pillar the ancient gateway to the sea;
And there comes o'er me, swift, resistless, free,
   Again that old fierce soul of storm and flood,
   With fire and joy exultant in the blood,
Erewhile through stormy years my destiny!

That strong voice of the sea, prophetic, great,
   How shall the weak of soul resist its call,
Having once loved it?   'T is the voice of fate,
   Swifter than tongue of siren to enthrall,
Such sway hath mighty nature o'er us still,
Such power, despise, deny her, as we will!

STARLIGHT SONG.

OVER the moonlit sea,
  Wafted from afar,
Floats sweet melody,
  Like a chant from a distant star,
Trembling upon the ear,
In cadence low and clear.

Over the haunted streams,
  Out of the isles of dusk,
Follow a breath and a sigh,
  Laden with rose and musk,
Like those which amid the years
Here bathed me in dreams and tears.

O voice long fled and far,
  That sang 'mid the haunted night!
Thou wert fleeter than spirits are
  That flee at the dawning light!
My beautiful mystical bride,
Who vanished ere starlight died,
  To chant 'mid the gleams of thy native streams,
  Where the heavenly isles abide!

THE COMING PREACHER.

HALF of the world, half of the schools,
　　A man combined of brain and brawn,
A workman wielding nature's tools
　　With vigor buoyant as the dawn.

A hearty nature, uncontrolled
　　By vices of restraint or pride,
Whose charities, like honest gold,
　　Ring standard in the market's tide.

One versed in philosophic lore,
　　And wisdom of the sects and creeds,
Yet holding them as but the door
　　To human nature's sacred needs;

With sympathies whose generous plan
　　No stinted meed of mercy brooks;
Who reckons learning less than man,
　　And human life as more than books.

Yet in whose free, far-circling thought,
  The graces that enrich and bless, —
All art, all science known and taught,
  Are parts of reigning righteousness.

To whom the fire and scourge of song,
  The spell that breathes from music's scroll,
The gleam that gilds the sculptor's throng,
  Are elements of endless soul.

A heart, — lo ! like a mother's, — soft,
  With deeps of unknown tenderness,
A spring of sacred joy, and oft
  Of sacred pity and distress !

Serene in spirit, unassailed
  By doubts that mar the soul's content,
In faith a giant, iron-mailed,
  Unshaken though the heavens be rent.

And his shall be the gaze to scan,
  Unquelled by surface waste of sin,
The deep mine of the heart of man,
  To find the gold that 's hid therein.

And having found it, his the hand
　To loose it from the rock and clod, —
Mould it, and stamp it with the brand
　And image of the Son of God.

And he shall come, and he shall be
　The help and healing of the time, —
The noble friend we look to see,
　The guide to heights we hope to climb!

GOD'S COUNTRY.

I.

DOST thou not know God's country, where it lies?
That land long dreamed of, more desired than
    gold,
Which noble souls, by dauntless hope made bold,
Have searched the future for with longing eyes!
Hast thou not seen in heaven its hills arise?
Hast thou not viewed its glories manifold,
'Midst sky-wide scenery splendidly unrolled,
Ripe for hearts' trust and godlike enterprise?
Yes, thou hast known it in familiar guise,
Its soil thy feet are keeping with fast hold;
And thou dost love its songs, its flowers dost prize;
Thy corn-land and thy wine-land is its mould:
'T is here, — 't is here God's land lies, the divine,
America, thy heart's true home and mine!

II.

All lands are God's lands; yet is this indeed
The home express of His divinity;
His visible hand redeemed it from the sea,
And sowed its fields with freedom's deathless seed.

He succored it most swiftly in its need;
In field and council men with awe did see
His arm made manifest almightily,
Scarce veiled in instruments of mortal breed.
He laid a way here for the feet that bleed,
A space for souls ayearn for liberty
To grow immortal in, — no more to plead
With nature for their portion which should be.
'T is here, O friend ! the land lies that shall grow
The vine of sacred brotherhood below.

THE FLIGHT OF THE WAR-EAGLE.

JULY 23, 1885.

THE eagle of the armies of the West,
Dying upon his alp, near to the sky,
Through the slow days that paled the imperial eye,
But could not tame the proud fire of his breast, —
Gone with the mighty pathos!   Only rest
Remains where passed that struggle stern and high;
Rest, silence, broken sometimes by the cry
Of mother and eaglets round the ravaged nest.
'T was when the death-cloud touched the mountain
          crest,
A singer among the awed flocks cowering nigh,
Looked up and saw against the sunrise sky
An eagle, in ethereal plumage dressed,
Break from the veil, and flame his buoyant flight
Far toward the hills of heaven unveiled and bright.

THE PARTING OF EMERSON.

Too fairy-light of keel, and swift of sail
To bide the winds and currents of the world,
At last good-by to fickle wave and gale!
Thy bark steers free, with all her wings unfurled,
Into the happy deeps, through foam-wreaths curled!
Thought, like a seraph, radiant at the peak,
Leans seaward through the shower of diamond
    spray
Tossed in light scorn from off the shallop's beak,
And at the helm Instinct, the pilot gray,
Guiding to golden islands of the day.

Speed on, bright sail, into the happy seas,
While vainly on the utmost line of strand
We wait to catch some faint breath of the breeze
That blows on thee from the enchanted land!

No more on bay or river-flood of ours
Shall thy evasive presence shift and shine,
Haunting our air with perfume of strange flowers,
And hinting of a grace and force divine,
Born of the breeze and odor of the brine!

GORDON.

'T is not so sad to know that thus he died,
Small power hath Death to trouble such as he,
Whom, overcome by darkest treachery,
No meaner pang than pity could betide,
But that so rich a spirit — such a pride
Of passion, splendor, immortality,
Such fire — be quenched and lost so utterly,
How sinks our heart of hope betrayed, belied !
Alas, and this is so ! Not all that zeal,
And power, and holy ardor could avail
To turn aside one mean assassin's steel !
What if within yon silent city's pale
All these imperial passions that we feel
Be found at last but splendid dreams that fail ?

EMERSON—CARLYLE.

ONE stood upon the morning hills and saw
The heavens revealed in symbol and in sign;
He read their mystic meanings, line by line,
And taught in light the reign of rhythmic law.
One in the twilight valleys, pierced with awe,
Beheld wan Hope amid great darkness shine, —
Saw gloom and glory blent without design,
And cried against a world of blot and flaw.
Sunrise and sunset poise the perfect day;
One was the prince of morning fair and free,
And one the lord of darkness was, and they
Made day and night one round of harmony,
For they were kings and brothers, and their sway
One law, — one new divine philosophy.

CHARLES DARWIN.

WHAT mind was this, that godlike and alone,
  Abode a season with us and is gone?
What eye was this, so keen, now dull as stone,
  That lit our world with prophesies of dawn?

Strange souls are sent us in this latter age,
  All brain and eye, enkindled not amiss,
Yet strong and bright and beautifully sage,
  But none more strong and beautiful than this.

They come and go among us scarcely seen,
  Wrapped in the mystic mantle of their thought;
We know them only after they have been,
  Then only know them by the work they 've
    wrought.

Clear souls from nature's secret realms estranged
  To teach awhile on earth what nature is,
The heavens which gave them take them, — they
    are changed,
  Their lives are changed, and none more changed
    than his —

Darwin's, who traced our nature to its germ
   Through all the dark entanglements of time ;
Who heard, from highest man to lowest worm,
   Life's long pulse beat in period and rhyme.

He bowed, and wrought, and listened hard, then
     rose, —
   Stood up and calmly spoke the truth he knew,
And standing thus in eminent repose
   Was changed, and passed serenely out of view.

Of all the simple and sublime of soul
   That Heaven has sent in wisdom's ministry,
To lead Thought's footsteps onward toward her
     goal,
   Was one more simple and sublime than he ?

PRESBYTERY.

ALONG the hushed aisles, little frequented,
　　Except by feet on sacred service bent
　　At Sabbath's hour of praise or sacrament,
The gathering pastors move with quiet tread.
Such men! see what a lion in that head!
　　What passion in those eyes magnificent!
　　What pride in that imperial brow unbent!
This face, what grace and subtle charm inbred;
What power divine, with what transforming rod,
　　Has tamed these fiery spirits into peace,
And made them reapers in the fields of God,
　　With naught of strength's decay or fire's decrease?
Love, heavenly master of all arts to bless,
And Love, that turns all hearts to tenderness!

SONG-SEEDS.

GATHER in the seeds of song,
Poet, while the year is mellow,
And the fields of God lie yellow,
In the sunshine warm and strong!
Gather in the goodly grain,
To the storehouse of the brain;
Fill the heart's deep granary
With rich increase, royally,
Brim their ample spaces o'er
With the season's choicest store;
Let the treasure-laden plains
Echo with the reapers' strains;
Fill the pleasant harvest ways
With the sickle's fiery blaze,
Get the pearl-seed of the dew
Where 't is nightly laid anew;
Win the pliant grace that plays
In the flag-leaves of the maize;
Catch the syllables that pass,
Whispering 'twixt the trees and grass;
In the garden watch an hour
For the soul of shrub and flower;

Ask the west-wind coursing fleet
For the charm of music sweet;
Woo the plaintive notes that fall
Through each dying interval.
Glean while genial light is here,
Winter cometh on apace,
When there 's need of singing cheer,
Winter's storm and gloom to chase,
Spirits blithe shall with thee go,
Where the richest harvests grow.

CONFESSION.

THOU art the friend and comrade, Poesy,
　　For whom I suffer all things, still content,
　　If not in vain for thee my light is spent,
The share of heavenly light that fell on me.
Thou art my meat, my drink, my liberty,
　　Thou art my garb, thou art my tenement,
　　Wherein I hide all night from floods unpent,
From lightnings, winds, and scourgings of the sea!
O thou art strong and lovely as the light,
　　Yea, as the light of morning strong and sweet!
Thou art the lover perfect in my sight,
　　Attending all my steps with eager feet,
The form, — the image in my dreams at night,
　　The morning glory that I rise to greet!

THE POET'S HERITAGE.

ALL riches, honor, fame's divine estate,
  Are due the gentle poet and his song.
  The earth is first for him ; to him belong
Life's every part and glorious aggregate.
To him the sweet birds carol soon and late,
  To him the streams run, and the fairy throng
  Of flowers live for his praises, and the strong
Sun and the sea roll tribute to his gate !
Men's trust is his, and childhood's innocent kiss,
  And love, and praise of women's gentle eyes ;
He passes greeting over the abyss
  With the heroic spirits of the wise, —
" How fares it with thee in the wilderness ? "
  " Bravely ! and how art thou in Paradise ? "

THOUGHT AND PASSION.

WHAT feeble and unhappy bards are we,
  Who trace our lines with over-cunning hand
  Upon a narrow strip of seashore sand,
Washed over night by strong floods of the sea!
We look at length and wonder where they be :
  They vanish, and we do not understand ;
  Not though we muse the verse divinely grand
Of him whose natural breath was poetry, —
Shakespeare the happy.   He with fearless art
  Sang all his deep heart forth, his lovely name
Is graved forever on the human heart.
  Our day is gracious, but our love is tame ;
We shrink from passion's face, and strive apart
  To kindle with cool thought the Muse's flame.

A SONG ON THE SHORE.

WELCOME, strong soul of Poesy, once more!
  O where so long hast thou been wandering?
  Thou comest to me like the gales of spring
That tell me winter's blasts are blown and o'er.
Since thou took'st sail and left me on the shore,
  Far vanishing as on a sea-bird's wing,
  I 've heard but steely tempests round me ring,
Crushed down 'neath ocean's mighty overpour!
Where wert thou? They did scourge me till my cry
  Outrang the tempest! yea, my soul was tried
Till angels saw and pitied me on high!
    They flew like doves and brought thee with the
      tide.
And now that thou art come joy hovereth nigh,
  Dimpling the deep with laughter far and wide!

WHIPPOORWILL.

LISTEN, how the whippoorwill,
From his song-bed veiled and dusky,
Fills the night ways warm and musky
With his music's throb and thrill !
'T is the western nightingale
Lodged within the orchard's pale,
Starting into sudden tune
'Mid the amorous air of June.
Lord of all the songs of night,
Bird unseen of voice outright,
Buried in the sumptuous gloom
Of his shadow-panelled room,
Roofed above by webbed and woven
Leaf and bloom by moonbeams cloven,
Searched by odorous zephyrs through,
Dim with dusk and damp with dew, —
He it is that makes the night
An enchantment and delight,
Opening his entrancing tale
Where the evening robins fail,

Ending the victorious strain
When the robins wake again.
Sacred bird, whom lovers bless
Strayed in love's charmed wilderness,
Couched in paradisial shade
By ambrosial branches made,
Or with passion-guided feet
Trailing paths through grass-beds sweet,
Over tufted sod and tangled
With moon-lilies pale bespangled;
Choice musician! loyal aid
To enamored youth and maid,
Parting with rich interlude
Mute-companioned solitude;
Dear interpreter to each
Of the thoughts too fond for speech,
Voicing with consummate art,
Secret thrill of heart to heart;
Subtle searcher, yet most free
Of insidious mockery,
Haunting every breath that strays
Through their love-bewildered ways,
Making all their dream and spell
One melodious miracle.

Spirit! from thy phantom bed,
Under the enchanted tree,
Say, what wooings hast thou sped
With thy songful sympathy?
What sweet hearts hast taught to thrill,
Whippoorwill, — ah, whippoorwill!

HELLAS.

'T is not where sculpture rules a world grown dim
  Fair Hellas lies, so dear to poet's heart, —
  Not in the galleries of sacred art,
Where group the old gods maimed in trunk and
     limb.
Nor is it where enchanted islands swim
  The warm Ægean waves, and where apart
  Through rosy mists Olympian heights upstart,
And float like dreams on the horizon's rim.
  Ah, where is Hellas then? 'T is where fresh eyes
  Look forth with love on nature's face again ;
There dreams spring up and fairy visions rise,
  And hallowed fanes appear by cliff and glen.
In the warm breast of Nature, Hellas lies, —
  Great mother of all gods and godlike men.

A TROPICAL SHOWER.

A PULSELESS languor lay upon the sea,
   The solemn mountains rested in their calm,
   The mighty forests slumbered, and the palm
Above the warm sands brooded breathlessly;
The heavens bent down in dark expectancy,
   Then suddenly the clouds burst 'midst the strain,
   Drenching the woods with torrents of warm rain,
Till in their deeps they roared tumultuously!
It ceased; — the sun broke forth with fire, and then,
   O how the birds sang! Such a joyous choir
Woke in the heart of hidden glade and glen
   As when a god immortal strikes his lyre
In deep Parnassian groves afar from men,
   'Mid smoke and incense from his altar fire.

SUMMER GODS.

WE were gods then, you and I,
On that June day long flown over,
When we lay amid the clover
As the gods were wont to lie.
The o'erbrimming sun did pour
Summer all our Eden o'er,
Richly from the fair blue sky
Sailing o'er us gloriously;
Stony mountains, skyward piled,
Took the sunny flood and smiled;
And the idle bay below
Warmed her bosom in the glow;
And a glamour of rich gold
Charmed the cedar arches old.
Heart of thine and heart of mine!
How we took it in like wine!
With our eager lips held up
Innocent to meet the cup,
Till the blood sang in the vein,
And the pulse played in the brain,
And the spirit sensitive
In her thousand springs did live!

How the golden overflow,
Turned away by laughing teeth,
Trickled to the chin below,
Staining all the beard beneath.
Ah, the glow in cheek and eye!
We were gods then, you and I.

Locks of jet, and locks of gold,
'Neath the rustic straw's rim straying, —
Winnowed plume and ringlet playing
Over foreheads bright and bold;
Eyes that roved the compass round
Of our royal pleasure-ground,
Like the bumblebees that reeled
In their drunken flight afield,
Lighting at a feast, to stay
But a moment, then away;
Limbs of Goth and limbs of Greek,
Turned with muscles round and sleek,
In a lawless grace dispread
O'er the warm crushed clover-bed;
Limbs that match their pliant might
With the mountain's stubborn height,
Conquering the cloven crest
Where the eagle hangs his nest;

Limbs that with elastic force
Lead the harvest's rhythmic course,
In a habitude that cleaves
To the sweet way of the sheaves:
'T was the blithe arcadian air,
In a plot with sun and breeze,
For a stolen season there
Throned us in Elysian ease.
Idle immortality!
We were gods then, you and I.

Oh the woodland mirth we made!
How the thunder of our laughter
Shook the scented cedar rafter
Of our columned long arcade!
Song-enchanted, reared behind,
With its echo leaf-enshrined;
How we shouted! how we sang!
How the shafts of wood-wit rang!
Till the cattle where they fed
Gazed with lofty-lifted head,
In a mild-eyed wonderment,
Mingled with their calm content,
Then with slow step circled nigh,
Pointed horn and gamesome eye,

And with antic fling and bound,
Hoofed it o'er the fragrant ground;
And the bee forgot the flower,
And the squirrel left his bower,
And the wingéd folks in pairs
Dropped around us unawares,
Once to listen to the mirth
Of the glad lords of the earth,
Wafts of precious cedar scent,
Balsam odor, breath of bee,
Smell of mint and clover blent
Blew through all our revelry, —
Arcady — oh, Arcady!
We were gods then, you and I!

THE NEW KINGDOM.

THERE is a kingdom in a rugged land;
  It lies between a mountain and a sea;
  A torrent roaring down in headlong glee
Divides it from a forest's ancient stand,
And in its narrow bounds by nature planned
  A happy monarch reigns in majesty;
  Though small his realm and few his subjects be,
Supremest powers obey his mild command;
And I, a pilgrim from a land forlorn,
  Find shelter there, and rest for weary feet,
  Welcome from fiery toil and desert heat
To genial feasts of royal wine and corn,
  The king and I together sit at meat,
And drink deep draughts from friendship's holy
     horn.

A DAY AND A FRIEND.

WE sat upon the shore, my friend and I;
   The lake lay rocking in the morning shine,
   Odors of gum were round us, and a pine
Played music while the waves danced, ceaselessly.
Joy of wild woods and waters and blue sky
   Flowed through our spirits like celestial wine;
   We talked of poet's hopes and thoughts divine,
And he was generous and I was shy.
O golden heart of all that golden day,
   Wise friend! so kind to my reluctant thought;
So gentle with the grace that went astray
   Through stammering speech and woodland ways
      untaught!
He read me by the things I dared not say,
   And loved me for the trust that doubted naught.

PHAON AND HYLAS.

In the growing months of spring,
Ere the days are long and yellow,
Runneth a young brook rioting
Through the meadow lowlands mellow;
Fed by copious dews and showers,
Free through wayward courses winding,
Rippling, trilling, brawling, laughing,
Air and wine of sunshine quaffing;
Haunts of birds and beds of flowers
Its enamored current finding;
Making cataracts in play,
Revelling in wreaths of sunlit spray
Where the pebbly shallows pave an undulating way;
Voicing joy in running measures,
Chasing pleasures, winning treasures,
Laughing scorn on moody leisures.
On it speedeth, shouting, singing,
Till the south-wind, hither winging,
Bringeth summer from the south,
Girt with flame and shod with drouth;
Then it faileth, then it drieth,
Dead in shallow pools it lieth,

Leaving but the echo of a lay
Wandering with the memories of happy yesterday.

Out of a rough rock's bosom year by year
 A mystic spring comes welling to the light;
'T is where a sheer cliff falls, with cedars near,
 Deep in the mountains out of common sight;
In a still pool its gathered waters sleep,
Rock-walled, and fringed with moss and ivies deep.

Fresh from the inmost mountain wells apart
 It breaks in splendor, singing as it flows
A chant for him who listens in his heart
 For one deep song to guide him as he goes, —
One pure, unfathomable thought of life
And beauty to make rich his years of strife.

I love the tripping song
Of the brook that all day long
Dances and laughs in the sun,
Ending when summer's begun
In the green and gold of the meadow.

But more I love that rock-born spring and pool
Of ceaseless, quiet water, deep and cool,
Within the mountain's dark and silent shadow.

THE SLAYER.

Ah, Poesy! thou glorious, deadly thing,
Fair to create and merciless to slay,
What have we done to thee, that day by day
Thou wearest us with fruitless suffering?
Is it for thine own glory thou dost wring
These souls with pangs that waste our hearts away,
This fairest web of life to fret and fray,
Weaving thereof our grave-clothes while we sing?
Thou art like Love, that wastes us in our spring, —
Or art thou Love's own self, though grown less gay,
That in this guise dost lead us still astray
And cheat us with the glitter of a wing?
I know not; only when I look I see
Toil paid with pain and faith with mockery.